Ovis
Has Trouble with School

written by Kelly Beins   Illustrated by Christine Tuccille Merry

BLUE MUSTANG PRESS

Blue Mustang Press
Boston, Massachusetts

First printing

ISBN 978-1-935199-25-0
PUBLISHED BY BLUE MUSTANG PRESS
www.BlueMustangPress.com
Boston, Massachusetts

Ovis
Has Trouble with School

written by Kelly Beins   Illustrated by Christine Tuccille Merry

Ovis
Has Trouble with School

written by Kelly Beins   Illustrated by Christine Tuccille Merry

Dear Reader,

The world of sensory processing can be a confusing place. 1 in 15 school-aged children experience sensory differences. Despite an advancing body of research and a quickly expanding body of knowledge, those children and families living with sensory differences often feel misunderstood, and at a loss for how to communicate to others what they are going through and what they need. I hope this book brings you connection...to your child, to your student, your client, or your friend. I hope you can find in Ovis, and in his family, a character to whom you can relate. In addition, I want these stories and pictures to spark a lightbulb (and a chuckle) that help you to see an everyday challenge that you or someone you love may have encountered, a little more clearly.

There is no medical diagnosis of sensory processing disorder. However, sensory challenges are a part of many existing diagnoses and regardless of diagnosis or "condition", our human experience makes us sensory beings. By reading to children we support various sensory systems and create a nurturing welcoming place for them to feel connected, both to themselves and to other people. This alone is a good place to start when trying to support a child with sensory processing differences.

I look forward to sharing more stories of Ovis and hope you will share with me, your stories of Ovis in your life!

Kelly Beins
Occupational Therapist (and sensory mom of a sensory kiddo)

Ovis doesn't like sheep school.

But Ovis isn't bad, he's just *bothered*.

bothered **by sounds,**

bothered **by his sheep skin,**

and *bothered* **by having to sit still all the time.**

Ovis doesn't like sitting still and not touching his friends.

He wants to *play*

and *move*.

Ovis likes it *quiet*, even though he makes *LOTS* of noise.

But everyone else follows the rules. Why can't he?

Ovis doesn't want to get in trouble.

So Ovis laughs….a lot!

Ovis rolls around on the floor…
…when he's not supposed to.

He plays when he *should* be working and talks when he *should* be listening.

SHOULD
SHOULD
SHOULD
SHOULD
SHOULD
SHOULD
SHOULD
SHOULD
SHOULD

Ovis thinks, "There sure are a lot of *shoulds* at school." Poor Ovis.

What's a little sheep to do?

Ovis's teacher knows someone who can help. Mrs. Sheep Dog, the O.T., has an idea. Mrs. Sheep Dog talks to Ovis, his parents, and the teacher.

"Ovis, tell the teacher how you feel."

"Say, my body feels B-A-A-D!" and see what she says.

So Ovis does.

When Shelley Sheep sits too close to Ovis, Ovis raises his hoof and says, "Teacher, I feel B-A-A-D!"

When Ovis gets too excited, his teacher lets him choose a green bean bag seat to lean on.

Green is Ovis's favorite color and really makes him happy.

When Ovis's skin itches or prickles, he raises his hoof and says, "My body feels B-A-A-D!"
Ovis's teacher gives him a small heavy blanket with stars on it to lay over his lap to help the itchies go away. Ovis likes stars too.

When Ovis feels wiggly and just can not sit still any longer, he says, "Teacher, this is B-A-A-D!"
His teacher lets him stand to color his picture instead of sitting.

Now Ovis is learning
to print.

Today's
Letter
Ss

He isn't afraid that he won't be able
to do it because now he gets to move around.

Sometimes Ovis tells
the teacher he feels bad
even when he
doesn't, because he doesn't want
to do what he is told.

But Ovis is learning that he is
only allowed to stand sometimes,
not ALL of the time;
the bean bag chair is just for
floor sitting or quiet reading time;
and he is learning that the
heavy little blanket actually
helps those itchies go away.

Other sheep want to try Ovis's blanket and seat and they want to stand up too,

so the teacher lets them, and Ovis shares… but not for keeps.

Ovis still goes to sheep school and green is still his favorite color. But now, when Ovis has a hard day, he knows what to do!

Ovis is learning that sheep school is not so B-A-A-D after all, and some days it can even be G-R-E-A-A-T!

SHEEP SCHOOL

www.ingramcontent.com/pod-product-compliance
Lightning Source LLC
LaVergne TN
LVHW061342060426
835511LV00014B/2068